The Money
Book
for Kids

The Money Book for Kids

by Nancy Burgeson

Illustrations by Aija Janums

Troll Associates

Library of Congress Cataloging-in-Publication Data

Burgeson, Nancy.
   The money book for kids / by Nancy Burgeson.
     p.   cm.—(A Troll survival guide)
   Summary: Readers learn ways to earn money, how to manage it, and
how to get and keep a job.
   ISBN 0-8167-2465-2 (pbk.)
   1. Finance, Personal—Juvenile literature. 2. Budgets, Personal—
Juvenile literature. [1. Finance, Personal.] I. Title.
II. Series.
HG173.8.B87 1992
332.024—dc20   91-15108

Money, Money, Money

Wouldn't it be nice if money grew on trees? Then, every time you needed some, you could just go out into the backyard and pick it.

Unfortunately, it doesn't work that way. You probably have to work or do chores to earn most of your spending money. And once you earn it, what do you do with it?

Run to the store and spend it as fast as you can?

Try to save a little but somehow it just flies away?

Managing money isn't really so hard. All it means is that you have to stop and think before you spend. Or maybe make a plan, either in your head or on paper, of how you want to use your cash.

That's what this book is all about. You and your money. How to earn it; how to take care of it.

It isn't about how to spend it. You already know all about that, don't you?

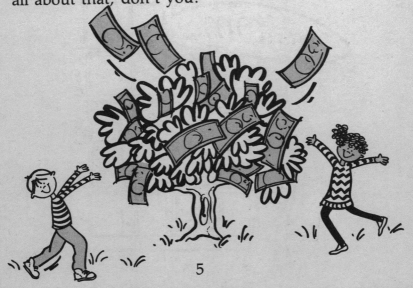

The Money Quiz

How smart are you about money? Take this little quiz and see. Answer the questions as *honestly* as you can.

1. If you want a new video, but your allowance is long gone, you
   a. wish on a star.
   b. beg and plead with your parents to help out.
   c. offer to mow the lawn in return for the cash you need.

2. When a neighbor asks you to baby-sit for the first time, you
   a. are too embarrassed to mention money, but hope you'll be paid.
   b. say in a nice way what you usually charge per hour.
   c. name a flat sum and hope the neighbor will be willing to pay it.

3. If you're going to a rock concert, you
   a. call ahead to find out what the tickets cost.
   b. hope you have enough money for a ticket.
   c. tell your friends to bring extra money in case you run short.

4. You've saved your money for weeks to buy the latest in boots, but your mother tells you you're throwing your money away. You
   a. don't buy the boots, but you're really disappointed.
   b. run out and buy the boots anyway.
   c. talk it over with your mom, explaining that you really want the boots, you've earned the money for them, you've thought it over, and you've decided to buy them.

5. You've been on a budget for three months and you've really been trying but you just can't seem to stick to it. So you
   a. make out a new budget, giving yourself a little more spending money.
   b. say the heck with it and stop trying to budget.
   c. force yourself to try again.

6. You're saving for that 10-speed bike you badly want, but then you see a super video game that you just have to have. You
   a. stop and think it over before you decide.
   b. blow most of your savings on the game.
   c. plead with your sister to loan you the money for the game.

7. You've made out a chart to see where your money goes and you see that you're spending

too much on snacks. You

   a. ignore the chart.

   b. ask your parents to increase your allowance.

   c. cut back on snacks.

8. You have a good job delivering papers, but some mornings you just don't feel like getting up so early. You

   a. get up and deliver the papers, but talk to your boss later about changing to an afternoon route.

   b. roll over and go back to sleep.

   c. yell for Dad to deliver the papers for you.

9. Granny sends you a big check for your birthday. You

   a. throw a party for your friends.

   b. make a list of the ways you would like to spend it.

   c. loan it all to your pal who's buying a new stereo.

10. You borrowed money from your brother to buy a tennis racket and you don't have enough to pay him back. You
    a. tell him you'll pay him back someday, but he has to wait.
    b. ask him to forget about the loan.
    c. arrange to do his chores to repay the loan or come up with a new schedule of repayment.

So how did you do? Below are the *best* ways to handle the situations described. Check your answers against these to see just how money-wise (or money-foolish) you are.

1. c	6. a
2. b	7. c
3. a	8. a
4. c	9. b
5. a	10. c

If you got 8 to 10 answers right, you're MONEY-WISE. Congratulations! You're well on your way to successful money management.

If you got 6 or 7 right, you're like most of the world—sometimes MONEY-WISE but in need of a bit of work on the money-management level. Don't worry, though. There's definitely hope for you!

If you got fewer than 6 right, you're MONEY-FOOLISH! You should be reading this book with a pencil and paper handy to jot down notes. Read on, and don't spend the rest of your life spending money foolishly.

Skinflint or Spendthrift?

A skinflint is a person who never wants to spend money. Another word for skinflint is miser (or cheapskate). A spendthrift is someone who spends money too freely and who winds up wasting it. Are you a spendthrift or a skinflint? Answer these questions below to find out.

ARE YOU A SKINFLINT?

	YES	NO
Is your money socked away?	☐	☐
Do you have to dust off your money before you buy anything?	☐	☐
Do your friends call you "Tightwad"?	☐	☐
Do you always try to get someone else to pay?	☐	☐
Do you disappear when the check arrives?	☐	☐

ARE YOU A SPENDTHRIFT?

	YES	NO
Are you always broke?	☐	☐
Do you treat your friends every time?	☐	☐
Is your allowance gone the day you get it?	☐	☐
When something new comes out, are you the first one to get it?	☐	☐
Does money burn a hole in your pocket?	☐	☐

If the answer to all of these (or most) questions in either column is yes, you could be in big trouble. Money trouble. It's better to be somewhere in between a skinflint and a spendthrift—enjoying the things money can buy, but knowing how to save, too!

Money Doesn't Grow on Trees

There are many ways to get money. Do you even realize where your money comes from? Think about it a moment. Does it come from any of these places?

► Mom and Dad when they're in the right mood.
► Gifts from relatives and friends.
► The tooth fairy.
► Allowance.
► Anybody who's around and who doesn't mind lending.
► A part-time job.

Allowance

Some kids get an allowance from their parents. That usually means a set sum of money given at a set time.

But watch out! Allowances can cause problems. Here are a few ways to avoid them.

► Work out with your parents how much your allowance should be. But how do you do that? One way is to ask your friends what their allowances are. (Tip: Don't just ask the richest kid you know. Your parents will figure it out in a jiffy!) Another way is to add up how much money you think you need each week. But don't get carried away. Usually, however, parents decide for themselves what they think is a fair allowance. But it never hurts to negotiate.

► Set a regular time for payment, like Saturday mornings. This will help you to budget your money—spending it over a certain period of time without going broke!

► Find out what chores go along with the allowance. Are you supposed to set the table or take out the garbage every night? Most parents insist that certain jobs be done around the house in return for allowance. Find out what they are and do them. That's your responsibility!

► Find out what the allowance is supposed to cover. For example, will Mom and Dad still pay for your school lunches and school supplies? What about family outings, like bowling, or popcorn when you're all at the movies?

► Try to discover whether your parents plan to use your allowance as reward and punishment. This is a little tricky. If you forget to practice the flute, or if you get a D in math, do you still get paid?

► Discuss with your parents their policy on advances. That means, can you borrow on next week's allowance? Say the music store is having a sale on tapes by your favorite group. The sale is for one day only. If Mom and Dad would give you next week's allowance this week, you could buy some tapes at a great price. So ask them.

How to Ask for a Bigger Allowance

Sometimes it seems like the more money you have, the more you spend. And prices just keep getting higher and higher. You just can't buy all the things you need. So, one solution is to ask Mom and Dad for a raise in your allowance. Here are some tips on how to do it. (P.S. Not all of them—maybe none—will work. You have to decide which way is best for you and your parents.)

► *Demand* a bigger allowance. Say it's your constitutional right. (WARNING: This one is risky and *not* recommended.)

► Use logic. Parents love logic. Be prepared. Ask for a reasonable increase. Show your parents a list of your expenses. Say you can't make ends meet. Say you need a cost-of-living raise. Who knows? They might buy it, if it's true.

► Tell them what your friends' allowances are. (WARNING: Most parents don't care what your friends' allowances are, so this could be risky, too.)

► Ask for a little more than you really need. This will give you some bargaining room.

► If all else fails, offer to do more chores. (Think carefully before offering this one!)

► Watch your timing. Try to catch your parents in a good mood. Don't pick the day Mom and Dad just paid the bills to ask for a raise. The day one of them got a promotion might be a good time, though.

► Don't ask too often. If your parents increased your allowance a month ago, they probably won't be willing to do it again so soon. Once a year is about right. Every six months, if you're desperate.

Borrowing Tips

The best advice ever given on borrowing and lending money was this: "Neither a borrower nor a lender be." William Shakespeare said that about 400 years ago, and it's still true today. But there are times when you might have to borrow or lend money. If so, remember this.

► Only borrow what you need. Why? Because you have to pay it back, of course.

► Be sure you understand exactly when the person you borrow from expects his money back. Especially if he's bigger than you are.

► If you need to borrow a big amount, maybe you can arrange to pay it back in installments. Or, instead of paying the loan back in cash, maybe you could pay it back by doing chores.

Lending Tips

If someone wants to borrow money from you, keep these things in mind.

▶ Has this person borrowed from you before and paid you back?

▶ Has this person borrowed from you before and *not* paid you back?

In a pinch, you can always quote Shakespeare.

12 Easy Ways to Earn Money

rake leaves
mow lawns *1.00*
shovel snow
baby-sit *1.00 hr.*
pet-sit
walk a dog
deliver newspapers
run errands *1.00*
wash windows
wax or vacuum floors *1.00*
help with laundry *.50*
wash cars *2.00*

More Ways to Earn Money

Bet you can think of lots more ways to earn money. List them here. Try to think of things you'd *like* to do. Be resourceful. There are a lot of interesting things you could do.

_____

_____

_____

_____

_____

_____

_____

Did you think of these? These are one-time specials.

► A lemonade stand. (Best in a busy area on a hot day.)

► A bake sale. (You have to bake the cookies and cakes, remember.)

► A yard sale. (A great way to get rid of old toys.)

Be sure to check with Mom and Dad before you start one of these projects.

Be Creative!

You can even create your own job. Start your own business. If you're extra good at something, use it.

▶ Do you like arts and crafts? Use your imagination! There are lots of things you can make that other people will find useful and attractive. Check out some how-to books for ideas.

▶ A young golfer could caddy at the local golf course.

▶ Or how about starting a house-cleaning service?

There are lots of creative jobs. See if you can think of a few that use your own special talents.

Where Are the Jobs?

▶ AT HOME: Ask your parents to help you find ways to earn money. There are always chores to be done. Or look around yourself. You can probably spot a job or two that somebody would be glad to hand over to you.

▶ ASK NEIGHBORS AND FRIENDS:
Pet-sit while the next-door neighbors are on vacation.
Take over a friend's baby-sitting job while she's at camp.
Shovel the snow from Mrs. Smith's driveway.
Ask around.

▶ BULLETIN BOARDS: Look at the bulletin boards in places like the supermarket and the bowling alley. There might be a job just right for you. Or put up a card of your own, offering your services.

▶ NEWSPAPER ADS: Check the ads in your local paper.

▶ JOB BANK: Is there one in your town? If so, see if you can get help with your job hunting.

▶ VOLUNTEER: Sometimes volunteering your services, such as at the local day camp, could lead to a paid job.

How to Get and Keep a Job

1. For your job interview, you wear
   a. any old thing.
   b. neat, clean, everyday clothes.
   c. your best party clothes.

2. You arrive at the interview
   a. ten minutes early.
   b. ten minutes late.
   c. right on time.

3. If you're supposed to mow Mr. Tyson's lawn, but you'd rather go to the ball game, you
   a. mow the lawn and forget the game.
   b. go to the game and forget the lawn.
   c. go to the game, but tell your sister to mow Mr. Tyson's lawn if she has time.

4. You mow Mr. Tyson's lawn and then find out you were supposed to trim the borders and rake up the grass as well. You
   a. demand more money.
   b. tell Mr. Tyson he's not being fair and you're going to tell your father.
   c. admit to yourself that it's your fault for not finding out *first* exactly what the job was.

5. If you can't baby-sit after 10 P.M. you
   a. hope the people you're sitting for won't be out late.
   b. hope Mom and Dad won't mind your getting home after your deadline.
   c. make sure the people you're sitting for know when you have to be home.

You don't need to be given the right answers for these, do you? You already know. The point here is to act responsibly. If you say you're going to be at a certain place at a certain time—be there! If you're supposed to do a certain chore on a certain day—do it! And always get all the important information *before* you agree to do something. That avoids confusion later.

Job Checklist

Review the following checklist when you're considering taking a job.

- ☐ Plan how many hours and which days of the week you can work.
- ☐ Make sure your job won't interfere with your studies.
- ☐ Make sure your job will allow you to spend some time with your friends.
- ☐ Check with your family to be sure your working hours won't conflict with family outings.
- ☐ Tell your employer about any family restrictions, such as what time you have to be home.
- ☐ Be sure to show up for work when you said you'd be there.
- ☐ Try not to cancel at the last minute.
- ☐ If you have to cancel, call and explain.
- ☐ Know the going rate of pay for the job and how much to ask for.
- ☐ Talk to your employer about how often you'll be paid and how.
- ☐ If the job is across town, find out if your employer plans to give you a ride.
- ☐ If you don't have a ride, arrange for transportation.
- ☐ Be sure you understand exactly what the job involves.
- ☐ Dress neatly.
- ☐ Be polite.
- ☐ Be on time.
- ☐ Don't be shy; if you have a problem, talk to your employer about it.

What Next?

So you have an allowance.

And a part-time job.

And a nice, big check on your birthday from Aunt Tilly.

So what's your problem?

Money worries!

You spent all your allowance on something you thought you wanted.

You don't know where the money you earned doing yardwork went.

Mom and Dad are nagging that you throw your money away on junk.

You're broke, there's a dance tomorrow night, and you don't have enough to pay the door fee.

How can you be sure this won't happen again?

Budget Time

You can *budget*.

That means you can learn to keep track of your money so you won't run short and miss a special outing.

It's not so hard.

First, try making a list of the things you spend money on.

Everything.

Then put a check by the ones you *can't* do without.

They're the essentials.

Here are some things, for a start.

You can keep adding your own personal items to the list.

☐ magazines
☐ snacks
☐ school supplies
☐ transportation
☐ music tapes and records
☐ books
☐ clothes
☐ accessories
☐ sporting goods
☐ hobbies

☐ cosmetics
☐ movies
☐ video games
☐ roller rink
☐ skiing
☐ dances
☐ rock concerts
☐ stereo
☐ bike
☐ trip somewhere special

_____

_____

_____

_____

_____

Figure It Out!

Now you can find out just what you're spending on all those things.

Every day, jot down how much you pay for each item you buy.

When you get your allowance or a money gift, or when you get paid, write that down, too.

Don't forget to write it down if you borrow money.

Money Earned	Money Spent (Item) (Cost)	Money Borrowed
Sunday		
Monday		
Tuesday		
Wednesday		
Thursday		
Friday		
Saturday		
Total	Total	Total

Planning a Budget

Now you're ready to make a money plan, or budget. First, decide what you want to allow yourself to spend on certain items, such as five dollars a week for snacks. Don't forget to leave something for emergencies.

If you want to save, make sure you have some money left over to put aside. Once you've got a plan, stick with it and give it a chance to work. You can always make changes if it doesn't. And if you need help, ask your parents for advice.

Expenses	How Much I Plan To Spend
Essentials	$
Extras	$
Emergencies	$
Savings	$

How Are You Doing?

Do you have any money left over at the end of the week?

Are you spending all your money on clothes, or snacks, or entertainment?

Do unexpected costs leave you with nothing but lint in your pocket?

Try keeping a chart for several weeks. That will give you an idea of how much money you usually have coming in (income) and how much you are spending (expenses).

	INCOME	EXPENSES (Essentials)	(Extras)
Week 1			
Week 2			
Week 3			
Week 4			

A Savings Plan

So you want to save some of your money, either for a special purchase or for a rainy day. Where are you going to keep your savings? That's up to you, but here are some possibilities.

► *In your pocket.* Then the money will be handy, but you could lose it. Cash in the pocket is also a temptation to spend.

► *Your parents could hold it for you.* This is a good choice, because the money would be available when you needed it, and it would also be out of the way of temptation. But you might want to be independent, and handle your money all by yourself.

► *A special place.* There are lots of places to keep money—under the mattress, in a piggy bank. It's up to you.

► *A savings account.* You can open your own savings account—or your parents could open it for you, or with you. You put your money in the bank, and the bank will pay you a small sum, called interest. The problem with a savings account is that the money is not easy to get to in a hurry.

Write here what you will do with your savings. Wait a few weeks and look at what you wrote. Do you still think it's a good idea? Or have you thought of something else already?

_____

_____

_____

_____

_____

_____

_____

_____